explaining
DEAFNESS

SARAH LEVETE

A+

Smart Apple Media

Smart Apple Media
P.O. Box 3263, Mankato, Minnesota 56002

U.S. publication copyright © 2010 Smart Apple
Media. International copyright reserved in all
countries. No part of this book may be reproduced
in any form without written permission from
the publisher.

Printed in the United States

Published by arrangement with the Watts
Publishing Group Ltd, London.

Library of Congress Cataloging-in-Publication Data

Levete, Sarah.
  Explaining deafness / Sarah Levete.
      p. cm. – (Explaining–)
  Includes index.
  ISBN 978-1-59920-313-3 (hardcover)
  1. Deafness–Juvenile literature. I. Title.
  RF291.37.L48 2010
  617.8–dc22

                                2008049289

Planning and production by Discovery Books
Limited
Managing Editor: Laura Durman
Editor: Gianna Williams
Designer: Keith Williams
Picture research: Rachel Tisdale
Consultant: Franklin Watts would like to thank the
    National Deaf Children's Society (NDCS) for their
    help in developing the information in this book.

Photo acknowledgements: Corbis: p. 12 (Bettmann), p. 30
(Bob Daemmrich), p. 34 (Louis Quail), p. 39 (Kat Wade/San
Francisco Chronicle); Exeter Royal Academy: p. 28; Getty
Images: p. 24 (First Light), p. 26 (Josh Bryant), p. 29 (David
McLain), p. 31, p. 37 (Karen Kasmauski/Science Faction);
Istockphoto.com: front cover bottom right (Oktay Ortakcioglu),
p. 9 (Oktay Ortakcioglu), p. 15 (Dustin Steller), p. 23, p. 25
(Andrew Howe); John Birdsall Photo Library/www.johnbirdsall.
co.uk: front cover top, front cover bottom left, p. 17, p. 19;
Photofusion: p. 35; RNID: p. 14; Science Photo Library: p. 18
(James King-Holmes), p. 21 (James King-Holmes), p. 38
(Anabella Bluesky); Synface: p. 33; Shutterstock: p.32 (Steve
Shoup)

Source credits: We would like to thank the following for
their contribution:
Patrick Hausmann story published courtesy of www.hear-it.org.
Angel Naumovski and Felicia Foinmbam stories published
courtesy of the NDCS. Evelyn Glennie story published courtesy
of http://www.evelyn.co.uk/live/hearing_essay.htm. Keith's
story courtesy of Keith Williams.

*Please note the case studies in this book are either true life
stories or based on true life stories.*

*The pictures in the book feature a mixture of adults and
children who are and are not deaf. Some of the photographs
feature models, and it should not be implied that they
are deaf.*

9 8 7 6 5 4 3 2 1

Contents

What is Deafness?

Sit still for a moment and listen. What can you hear? Perhaps your teacher talking to another student, the buzzing of a computer, your mother talking on the phone, or a pencil scratching over paper as a friend writes?

A person who is totally deaf will not hear anything. If a person is profoundly deaf, he or she will hardly hear anything. Someone who is hard of hearing may hear some muffled sounds, a bit like hearing sounds from the bottom of a swimming pool.

How Many People are Deaf?

According to the World Health Organization, there are about 278 million people worldwide with moderate to profound hearing loss in both ears.

There are nearly 4.8 million people in the U.S. who are deaf, partially deaf, or hard of hearing. Many of these are young people. You may be deaf or hard of hearing, or you may have a friend or relative who is.

Different Challenges

Being deaf presents different issues and challenges for each individual. How deafness affects people depends on several factors, such as the extent of deafness, when and how the person became deaf, and the support offered to that person.

Degrees of Deafness

There are different degrees of deafness and these are most often classified as mild, moderate, severe,

LEVELS OF DEAFNESS

Mild Deafness Can hear a baby crying or music from a stereo, but may be unable to hear whispered conversation.

Moderate Deafness Can hear a dog barking or telephone ringing, but may be unable to hear a baby crying.

Severe Deafness Can hear a chainsaw or drums being played, but may be unable to hear a piano or a dog barking.

Profound Deafness May hear a semi truck or airplane noise. However, this level of deafness also stretches to include those who are totally deaf and cannot hear anything.

or profound. Few people are totally deaf. Most deaf people can hear some sounds at certain pitches and volumes. There are some people who have little or no hearing in one ear, and ordinary levels of hearing in the other. This is known as unilateral deafness. Deafness does not always fit into a particular category, for example a person might have a moderate to severe hearing loss.

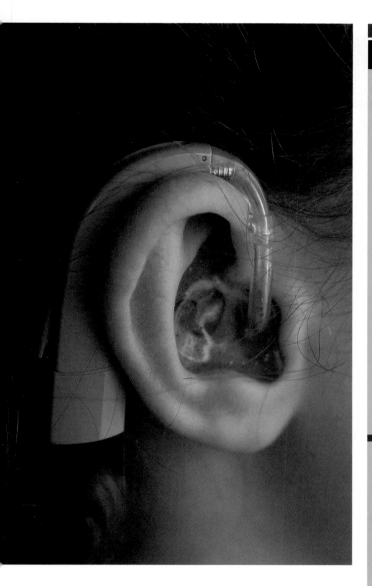

▲ *Deafness can affect anyone and to any degree. This girl can hear with the help of her hearing aid. Others who are profoundly deaf are only able to hear very few sounds.*

Deafness is sometimes called a hearing impairment, but some people object to this because the word "impairment" suggests that something needs to be fixed or corrected. They believe that being deaf is not a disability, but is about belonging to a cultural and linguistic group (see page 36-37).

TRUE OR FALSE?

Read these statements and decide which is true or false. Check your answers below.

1 All deaf parents have a deaf child.
True or false?

2 All deaf people can lip-read everything.
True or false?

3 A deaf person can hear if you shout.
True or false?

4 Bright clothes and jewelry make it harder to lip-read. *True or false?*

5 Deafness and intelligence are not connected.
True or false?

Answers

1 False. A deaf parent may have a hearing or a non-hearing child (see pages 14-15).

2 False. A person (deaf or hearing) can learn to lip-read, but many words make the same shape when spoken. This makes it hard to understand everything by lip-reading alone (see pages 22-23).

3 False. It helps a person who has some hearing if you speak clearly, but shouting does not make the sounds clearer and it is uncomfortable for someone wearing a hearing aid.

4 True. Bright colors can distract a lip-reader from looking at a person's mouth (see pages 22-23).

5 True. A person who is deaf can be as intelligent as anyone who is not deaf.

Ears and Sounds

We hear sounds through our ears. The ears then send messages to the brain, which interprets the sounds.

How the Ear Works

The ear consists of three main parts—the outer ear, middle ear, and inner ear.

The main part of the outer ear is made of a bony material called cartilage and a softer ear lobe, both of which make up the pinna. The pinna is cup-shaped to help collect sound waves.

▼ *This diagram shows how sound travels through the ear.*

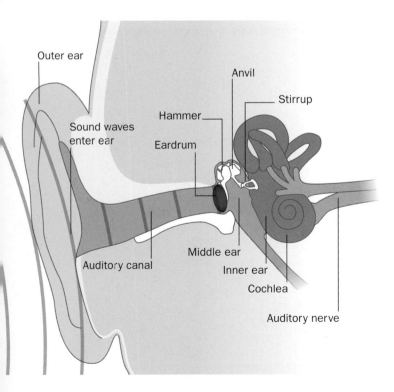

Outer ear
Sound waves enter ear
Hammer
Eardrum
Anvil
Stirrup
Auditory canal
Middle ear
Inner ear
Cochlea
Auditory nerve

The auditory canal, also known as the hearing or ear canal, travels from the outer ear towards the middle ear.

The middle ear is the space between the eardrum and inner ear and it is filled with air. The eardrum is a thin membrane that stretches across the auditory canal. Attached to the eardrum are the ossicles, the three smallest bones in the body—known as the hammer, anvil, and stirrup—which lead into the inner ear.

The inner ear is a maze of liquid-filled tubes and spaces and contains the cochlea, which is a snail-shaped bony tube filled with liquid. Inside the cochlea is the Corti, the hearing organ. This is covered in over 20,000 tiny hair sensors or cells. The auditory nerve leads from the inner ear towards the brain.

Waves of Sound

Sound is a form of energy. When you make a noise, invisible vibrations or waves of sound travel through the air. Sound waves travel from the source of the sound through the outer ear into the air-filled auditory canal and towards the middle ear. As the waves hit the eardrum they make it vibrate. In turn, these vibrations make the ossicles move. The movements reach a thin layer of tissue called the oval window. As this responds to the vibrations, it creates waves through the fluid in the cochlea, making the hair cells move. The hair cells change the movement from the sound waves into electrical impulses or signals. These electrical signals travel along the auditory nerve to the brain where they are understood and translated as sounds that you hear.

Having two ears helps you work out the source of a sound. If a sound comes from the right, for instance, it will reach your right ear slightly sooner than your left ear.

High and Low

Sounds are either high or low—this is called the pitch. The pitch of a sound depends upon the frequency of the sound waves. High frequency sound waves are close together because there are

more sound waves per second. Low frequency sound waves are further apart because there are fewer waves per second. Frequency is measured in Hertz (Hz). The volume of a sound is measured in decibels.

▼ *The large wave diagram shows how sound is measured. The smaller diagrams show waves at two different frequencies. The second wave is twice the frequency of the first, so the sound has a higher pitch.*

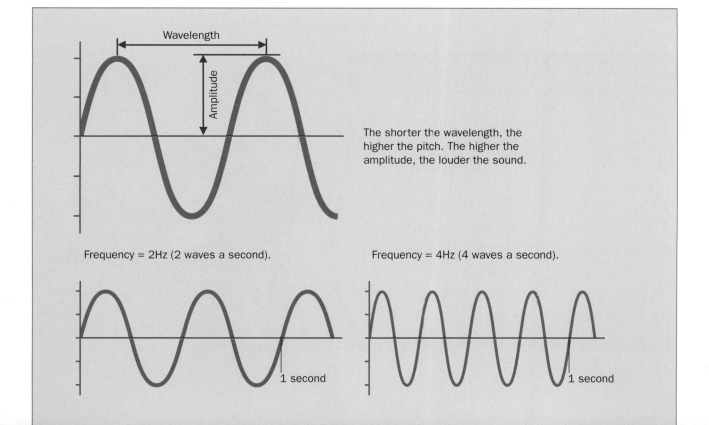

Wavelength

Amplitude

The shorter the wavelength, the higher the pitch. The higher the amplitude, the louder the sound.

Frequency = 2Hz (2 waves a second).

Frequency = 4Hz (4 waves a second).

1 second

1 second

Types of Deafness

More people become deaf than are born deaf. People who were born hearing and become deaf are often described as "deafened." Their deafness may be sudden, due to injury or illness, or it may be a gradual process.

Temporary and Permanent Deafness

Deafness can be a permanent or a temporary state, depending on the cause. For instance, a build-up of sticky earwax can block sound waves from traveling along the auditory canal, causing temporary hearing loss. A syringe is used to get rid of the wax, and hearing is restored. However, for many people, deafness is permanent—it does not disappear. Deafness caused by blockage or interference from the outer ear to the inner ear is called conductive hearing loss. This can be permanent or temporary. Sensorineural or nerve hearing loss is caused by a fault in the inner ear, often involving the hair cells, or the auditory nerve. This deafness is permanent.

From Mild to Profound

The level of deafness is defined by the quietest sound a person can hear. This is measured in decibels. The quietest sounds a person with mild deafness can hear are between 25-30 decibels,

▼ *This portrait from 1892 shows Helen Keller, age 12, with her teacher, Anne Mansfield Sullivan.*

HELEN KELLER (1880–1968)

When she was 18 months old, Helen Keller became seriously ill. As a result she became both blind and deaf, known as deafblind. Until Helen was seven years old, she was frustrated because she could not communicate with those around her. Helen's parents hired a teacher and she learned to speak by feeling her teacher's mouth as she spoke. Helen wrote many books, gave lectures, campaigned for disability rights, and inspired many people.

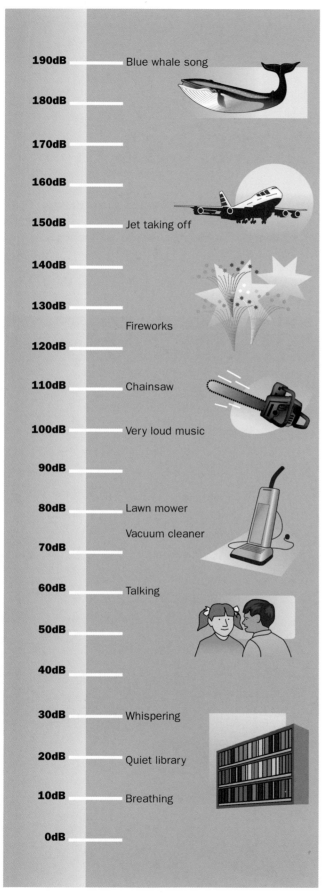

190dB	Blue whale song
180dB	
170dB	
160dB	
150dB	Jet taking off
140dB	
130dB	
	Fireworks
120dB	
110dB	Chainsaw
100dB	Very loud music
90dB	
80dB	Lawn mower
	Vacuum cleaner
70dB	
60dB	Talking
50dB	
40dB	
30dB	Whispering
20dB	Quiet library
10dB	Breathing
0dB	

approximately the volume of a clock ticking. People with mild deafness may find it hard to hear conversations clearly when there is lots of other noise. A person who is profoundly deaf can usually only hear sounds of 100 decibels or more (the sound of very loud music).

Tinnitus

Have you ever heard a ringing noise after hearing very loud music? The noise usually disappears. But for many people, this ringing, whistling, or buzzing noise does not go away. This is a condition called tinnitus. It is estimated that there are 12 million people permanently affected by tinnitus in the United States. The unpleasant noises can be constant or intermittent. Tinnitus makes sleep difficult and people can find it hard to concentrate or to hear conversations which are drowned out by the ringing noises.

There are many different causes of tinnitus, including ear infections, objects or growths in the ear, or wax build-up. Loud noise can permanently damage the cochlea, in the inner ear, and this can also result in tinnitus.

Different Issues

If a child or adult loses some or all hearing, he or she can use the previous experience of the spoken word to develop and continue spoken and heard communication. A person who is born deaf has no experience of hearing speech and finds it harder to develop any spoken language.

◀ *This chart shows the volume of certain sounds, measured in decibels.*

Causes of Deafness

A childhood illness, old age, or constantly listening to a very loud personal music player can all cause deafness. There are many reasons why a person is or becomes deaf, and these can occur at any stage in life.

Before Birth

One or two babies in every thousand are born with some type of deafness. This may be due to the baby's genes, which are inherited from its parents. Genes are the building blocks of an individual's physical makeup, determining which characteristics are inherited. Deafness can be inherited from either parent or even a grandparent. If a pregnant woman catches an infection, such as rubella, this can pass to the growing fetus in the womb, and this sometimes causes deafness in the baby. Difficulties at birth can also cause deafness. If a newborn baby does not receive enough oxygen, its brain cells can be damaged. This can cause hearing problems because the brain is unable to process the electrical signals sent through from the auditory nerve.

Conductive Deafness

Conductive deafness is the most common type of deafness. It occurs when sound cannot pass through the outer and middle ear to the cochlea and auditory nerve in the inner ear. Causes of conductive deafness include a perforated eardrum,

▶ *These flat pack earplugs are easy to assemble. They are designed for young people to use at nightclubs or gigs.*

TRENDY EARPLUGS

Concern is growing about the number of young people suffering from hearing loss because of listening to very loud music (over 85 decibels) at clubs and parties. The Royal National Institute for the Deaf (RNID), based in England, is running a campaign called "Don't Lose the Music," which encourages people to wear earplugs to protect their hearing. The earplugs they recommend reduce the volume, not the quality of the sound. The RNID is looking at producing specially designed earplugs that will become a fashion accessory that people do not mind wearing.

"If you slather on sunscreen or wear a bike helmet when you ride, why not wear earplugs and protect your ears from the risk of permanent damage?" Emma Harrison, RNID's Head of Campaigns.

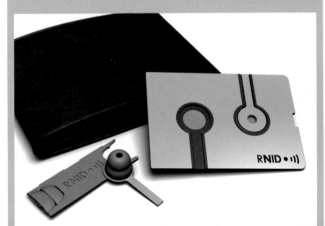

either pierced by a sharp object or damaged by a very loud noise. Glue ear also commonly causes temporary deafness in children. This occurs when fluid builds up in the middle ear, preventing the movement of sound waves to the inner ear. Glue ear can either clear up naturally after a short period of time, or it can develop into a long-term condition requiring surgical intervention. The fluid is drained from the ear and little tubes are put inside the eardrum. These stop any more fluid building up.

Sensorineural Deafness or Nerve Deafness

As sound passes through the outer and middle ear, the tiny hair cells in the cochlea convert sound waves into electrical signals (see page 11). These signals travel along the auditory nerve to the brain. Most cases of sensorineural deafness are caused by loss of, or damage to, the hair cells in the cochlea. This type of deafness can be genetic, or may be caused by an infectious disease such as rubella, mumps, measles, or meningitis, and is permanent. The term "mixed deafness" is often used when someone has a mixture of conductive and sensorineural deafness. This means that a person's deafness is caused by more than one problem.

In old age, the inner ear begins to wear out and the tiny hair cells do not work as well as they used to. This often causes deafness in elderly people.

Otosclerosis

Hearing loss can also be caused by a condition called otosclerosis. The middle ear bone hardens or grows abnormally, preventing the ear from working

▲ *Listening to your favorite music played loudly on an MP3 player can damage your hearing over time.*

properly. Otosclerosis can be hereditary, which means it runs in certain families.

Damaging Noise

People usually wear protective earmuffs when they operate very noisy machinery or equipment, such as a pneumatic drill which can produce noises over 90 decibels. Over a long time, exposure to very loud noises can damage the sensitive hair cells in the inner ear. Even listening to a personal stereo too loudly or regularly going to a nightclub where very loud music is played can cause deafness – temporary or permanent, partial or complete. If a noise makes it difficult to talk to a friend at a distance of about 6 feet (2 m), then the noise is loud enough to damage your hearing.

Signs of Deafness

You cannot usually tell if someone is deaf or hard of hearing just by looking at them.

A person who is deaf looks just like anyone else.

Detecting Deafness

Although most countries have tests to detect deafness (see pages 18–19), many children go through their early years without anyone realizing they have a hearing difficulty. Often children themselves are not aware that they cannot hear clearly. Many older people develop ways to cover up or cope with deafness, perhaps because they do not want to admit that there is a problem.

It is easier to detect total or profound deafness. For instance, a person who is totally deaf will not respond to sounds such as clapping hands or a door slamming.

When signs of deafness are picked up early on, particularly with children, it means they receive the support needed to develop and improve communication skills.

COPING WITH TINNITUS

Keith developed tinnitus when he was 16 years old. "I remember noticing a ringing in my ears, like we all get after listening to loud music, but it wouldn't stop. Then it kept getting worse. It sounded like radio static combined with a whistling kettle noise. I just remember being really worried about it and at first it drove me crazy. The only way to get away from the noise was to sleep, but it was hard to get to sleep! In the end I realized I just had to deal with it or it would take over my life. So I thought about the noise as if it were just the sound of the ocean in the background, a kind of comforting noise."

Signs in Children

These are some signs that a child may have difficulty hearing, but it is important to remember that these signs can also be caused by many other things.

For example, a child:
- only notices other people when they can be seen, (though shadows, vibrations, other people's faces, and sometimes even smell can make a deaf person realize that someone is near them)

- has not learned to speak when most other children of the same age have done so

- seems to speak differently from other children of a similar age

- lacks concentration at school (although this can be caused by lots of other reasons)

- turns up the TV too loud

- does not get involved in conversations

- seems isolated from others

- often asks for things to be repeated

- answers questions with unrelated answers.

Feeling Isolated

Imagine some friends are chatting, the radio is playing music in the background, and the washing machine is whirring and rumbling. You try to follow what is being said, but the sounds are too muffled for you to follow the conversation clearly. No one seems to notice that you are not involved in

▲ *Joining in conversation is hard if you cannot hear clearly and deafness has not been diagnosed.*

the chat. Perhaps they just think you are being a bit moody or unfriendly. This can be very frustrating and can make you feel isolated. This is how it feels to someone who is hard of hearing, but who has not received a diagnosis or support.

At school, a child may be easily distracted and lose interest in lessons, because he or she cannot hear clearly what the teacher is saying. The teacher may think that the child is disruptive and rude and not interested in learning.

Diagnosis

There are many tests to diagnose deafness. These range from simple tests, such as whispering behind a person's ear, to using computers and recording equipment to find out what happens inside the ear. Different tests are used for people of different ages.

Testing Babies and Children

Babies usually have routine tests to check their hearing. In a test called an otoacoustic emission, an audiologist (see page 19) puts a small earpiece linked to a computer and microphone in a baby's ear and plays a clicking sound. If the cochlea works properly, the earpiece picks up the response of the cochlea and this is recorded on the computer.

In another test, small sensors and headphones measure what happens to the cochlea, the auditory nerve and the brain when a sound is heard.

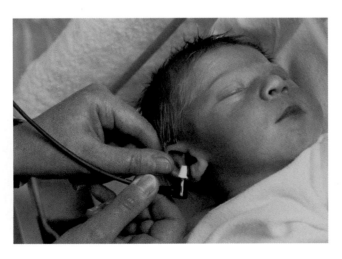

▲ *Some hearing tests, such as this otoacoustic emission hearing test, can be carried out on tiny babies, even as they sleep.*

Toys and games can be used to test older children's hearing. The child is asked to move a toy each time he or she hears a certain noise. If the child does not do this, it is unlikely he or she can hear the sound.

Detailed computer pictures of what happens inside the body, called MRI scans, can show the extent of any brain damage that may cause deafness.

"Late diagnosis can have a devastating effect on language acquisition, communication development, confidence, and social skills which can last a lifetime. However, if deaf children are identified at an early stage, and appropriate support is given, research shows there is no reason why they cannot develop at the same rate as their hearing peers."
Deafness Research, UK

Audiograms

Results of a hearing test are printed onto a chart called an audiogram. This shows how loud a sound must be for the child to hear it and the frequency of the sound. Some people can only hear high frequency sounds and others can only hear low frequency sounds (see page 11). Information from the audiogram helps an

▲ *During this hearing test, the audiologist plays sounds to the girl through a pair of headphones. When the girl hears a particular sound, she responds by pressing a button.*

AUDIOLOGISTS

An audiologist is a specialist in hearing difficulties. He or she runs hearing tests and helps to fit hearing aids (see pages 20-21). Often an ear, nose, and throat doctor is also involved in diagnosing deafness and finding the cause. Finding out the cause of deafness helps the audiologist decide which treatment may be appropriate.

audiologist to make sure the individual has the best hearing aid (see page 20) for their ears, should they decide to have one.

(see pages 20-21)

CASE NOTES

FELICIA'S STORY

Felicia Tendo Foinmbam, who lives in Kenya, has three deaf children. Her first child was not diagnosed as profoundly deaf until he was about five years old. His teacher noticed that he did not respond to any requests or instructions. It took Felicia some time to find a hearing center where her son's hearing could be tested. Felicia says:

"Learning that our children were deaf has brought about varied emotions at different times. The feelings of shock, embarrassment, inadequacy, confusion, and worry, on how to cope with the enormous task, were immediate.

Learning more about deafness really helped me to cope and I have really tried hard to come to terms with the problems that my children face, as well as making sure that I am strong so that my children are not affected emotionally. Above all I have tried to find out how I can give them the best education possible.

The children were diagnosed late because there were no early assessment and audiological facilities, and because my family reassured me that everything would be OK and there was no need for a test. This has meant that the help I can give my children to develop language also started late."

Treating Deafness

Sometimes deafness can be cured. For instance, a course of antibiotics can clear up an ear infection that blocks the middle ear. When the infection goes, hearing returns. Doctors can also mend damaged eardrums and even create "bionic ears."

Hearing Aids

Hearing loss can be treated with a hearing aid which amplifies sounds. A hearing aid consists of a built-in microphone that picks up sound waves. The hearing aid turns the sound waves into electronic signals that vary according to the pattern of the sound. These electrical signals are sent to a tiny loudspeaker. This converts them into louder sounds which are sent to the microphone on the hearing aid. However, as well as enabling a person to hear speech more clearly, the hearing aid also amplifies other sounds at the same time. For this reason, a hearing aid can be turned on and off.

Digital hearing aids convert sounds from a microphone into data or numbers. A tiny computer in the hearing aid converts these back into sounds. Digital hearing aids are set so that background noise can be minimized and only the types of sounds that a person needs to hear, such as speech, are amplified.

Sound and Bone

Bone can carry sound. Some hearing aids, called bone anchored hearing aids, use bone to conduct and amplify sounds instead of the air inside the auditory canal and middle ear. These hearing aids bypass the ear canal and middle ear if they are damaged. Instead, sound is sent through an implant just behind the ear. It passes through the skull bone to the cochlea and then through the auditory nerve to the brain.

Cochlear Implants

For some profoundly deaf people, a hearing aid will not work because they cannot hear enough sound

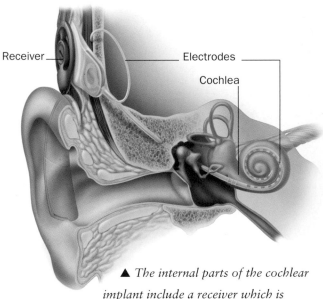

Receiver — Electrodes

Cochlea

▲ *The internal parts of the cochlear implant include a receiver which is placed directly under the skin and a multi-electrode wire array, which is inserted into the inner ear (the cochlea).*

to be amplified. However, many profoundly deaf people can hear with special implants known as cochlear implants. These are tiny devices, the size of a coin. One part of the device is a microphone and speech processor (worn outside the body, often near the ear) which captures sounds and converts them into digital signals. The processor sends these signals to a receiver just under the skin, which in turn sends the signals to implanted electrodes in the cochlea. Here the signals are turned into electrical signals and then translated by the brain into sounds.

Implant Problems

Many people with cochlear implants hear a range of sounds, from the sound of the television to the telephone ringing. Young children in particular benefit from cochlear implants because it helps them to develop and understand speech patterns from an early age. However, not everyone with a cochlear implant has their hearing improved. Some people begin to experience tinnitus (see page 13), and as with any operation, there are some risks such as causing damage to facial nerves, though this risk has been reduced with new surgical procedures. The operation is also expensive.

PATRICK'S STORY

From the age of 17, Patrick Hausmann was a DJ at private parties and in clubs. Today, at age 24, he works as a taxi driver.

Patrick worked as a DJ almost every weekend. "I never took special precautions. If the noise didn't reach almost to the threshold of pain, it wasn't cool. I reached the point where my ears always hurt after a night on the town."

After a New Year's celebration, a firework exploded close to him. From then on, Patrick began to hear high-pitched noises in his right ear. He thought this tinnitus would go away: "I just wanted to put it out of my mind, hoping that my hearing would get better. I kept working and took on even more gigs. Turning records allowed me to forget about my hearing problem and concentrate on the music."

His girlfriend had to repeat everything she said to him, but it took Patrick a year before he saw a hearing specialist. "I thought hearing loss was only for old people." He was sad and frustrated when the doctor told him that he had suffered hearing loss in both ears.

Today, Patrick wears a hearing aid. This, too, took some getting used to. He worried that everyone could see it. But he soon realized that the hearing aid made normal conversations possible for him. Now, the hearing aid has become part of his life. "It's like glasses; at some point you don't even notice that you are wearing it."

◀ *A girl with a cochlear implant is tested by an audiologist. She must place a ball on a frame when she hears noises.*

Lip-Reading

Silently say *dog*, *cat*, and *mouse*. Notice how the shape of your lips and tongue changes for each word. Deaf people (and others) can often read a person's lips to understand what is being said.

Lip-reading is "seeing" the sound of speech by reading words from lip shapes, facial expressions, and hand gestures. Many people who are deaf use their lip-reading skills to help them understand spoken words. For some totally deaf people, lip-reading is the only way to understand the spoken word.

Sounds such as *sh* and *ch* are made using similar mouth shapes. Some words, such as "hat," "sat" and "cat" all have the same mouth shape when spoken, so lip-reading is usually supported by visual and facial gestures. It is quite a skill to lip-read and many communities run lip-reading classes.

Sometimes experienced lip-readers are used in legal trials. They "translate" any mouth actions caught on CCTV cameras and these transcripts can be used as evidence.

Tips to Help You Lip-Read

• find a quiet place for the conversation

• ask the speaker to face the light

• ask for things to be repeated or said in a different way or ask the speaker to stop if you miss something

• watch the speaker's whole face, not only the lips. Facial expressions and gestures will tell you a lot about what is being said

• take notes if you need to.

Tips to Help Someone Lip-Read You

• face the light when speaking

• introduce the topic of conversation

• speak clearly, neither too fast or too slow

• do not shout—it actually makes it harder to read the shapes your lips are making

• use natural facial expressions, gestures and body language

• avoid wearing bright jewelry or clothes that can distract the lip-reader

• avoid touching your face

• repeat or rephrase if the lip-reader is unclear.

Lip-Speaking

Sometimes, a lip-speaker is used to help someone lip-read. The lip-speaker silently repeats what a person has said, clearly shaping the words and repeating the flow, rhythm, and phrasing of natural

speech as used by the person talking. A lip-speaker also uses facial expressions, natural movements, and finger spelling if requested (see page 25) to help the lip-reader.

▲ *Lip-reading is a skill that helps deaf people understand the spoken word. Not all deaf people can lip-read.*

Sign Language

Sign language is a language of movement. It is based on a complex combination of hand movements, arm movements, and gestures that represent ideas and words. There is no single international sign language—many countries have their own language, but they share several common signs.

A History of Sign Language

One of the first people to promote the use of sign language was Charles-Michel De l'Épée in the eighteenth century. This French priest met two deaf sisters who used a system of signing to communicate. This inspired De l'Épée to set up a shelter for deaf people, which then became a school for sign language. The idea of sign language soon spread across Europe and to America. In the United States, American Sign Language (ASL) is the fourth most common language. British Sign Language (BSL) is recognized in the United Kingdom as a minority language, along with Welsh and Gaelic.

American Sign Language

Over 500,000 people in the United States communicate with ASL. Many deaf people in Canada and Mexico also use ASL. ASL is not related to spoken or written English because it has its own grammar and structure. People use their hands, facial expressions, and body motions to convey meaning when they converse in ASL. Because it is a mainly visual language, most ASL

▶ *Just like learning any language, it can take a while to become fluent in sign language.*

NICARAGUAN SIGN LANGUAGE

Until the 1970s, there was no sign language in Nicaragua. There were hardly any schools where children who were deaf could work and meet. Deaf children probably developed signs to communicate with their family and friends, but there was no one sign language. Then, several schools for special education were built. Deaf children were able to meet with each other regularly. Over ten years, the children developed a sign language which they passed onto their children. Nicaragua now has its own sign language.

users tend to write in English. Just like spoken languages, sign language changes and evolves with the people who use it. Some signs can vary from region to region. The age and ethnicity of the users also creates variety in ASL.

▼ *American signs for the letters A, B, C, and D.*

Manually Coded English (MCE)

Speaking and signing at the same time is called Manually Coded English (MCE). For example, people who know a few signs may attempt to converse with someone who is deaf by using the signs in place of the English words. MCE has no relationship with ASL because it instead follows the grammar of the English language. It's not considered a sign language because it's only a "manual form" of language.

Finger Spelling

Finger spelling spells out words using hand movements that represent each letter of the alphabet. It is often used alongside sign language to spell out the names of places or people, to spell words when there is no sign, or to spell a word the signer does not know the sign for. In American finger spelling, only one hand is used to sign the letters. Generally, people use sign language instead of finger spelling because it takes a long time to spell out each letter in a word.

Deafness and Education

There are many schooling options for deaf children. They can attend schools that are for deaf children only, while many attend mainstream, public schools. Each type of school offers different benefits.

Public schools

At a public school, a deaf child mixes with mostly hearing children. Some public schools have special units, where children are taught with the help of a signer or interpreter. Because teaching is mainly spoken, deaf children (depending on their level of deafness) may need some support. This may be a note-taker or a signer who can translate the spoken word. Some children with limited hearing use their lip-reading skills and hearing aids.

Reading Phonetically

Today, many schools teach children to read phonetically, by sounding out a word. This is very hard to learn without any hearing or experience of hearing. Consequently, many deaf children find it difficult to learn to read with this new system.

Continuing Controversy

Some people believe that public schools help deaf children learn how to communicate in a hearing world. Others argue that the child is often left out of social activities and that his or her education is more difficult. For this reason, many deaf children attend special schools for the deaf (see pages 28-29).

"Deaf people can do anything except hear."
Irving King Jordan, the first deaf president of Gallaudet University, USA

◀ *This boy, who is deaf, signs at his public school in Tattershall, UK. All of his classmates have learned sign language, too.*

TYRONE'S STORY

Tyrone Givans is profoundly deaf and attends a mainstream [public] school with a deaf unit.

"I have been deaf all my life. I'm the only deaf person in my family, so sometimes it's hard for me to understand. The best thing about my school is that I have quite a lot of friends, and that helps me a lot. I teach them how to do sign language because if I don't understand something and then someone repeats it in sign language, it makes sense.

When I first started my mainstream class it was quite difficult. When I was in fourth grade, some people bullied me. Now the other children treat me like a normal hearing person.

When I am in my unit class, my teachers help me and I can do a lot of work. When I go to my mainstream class with all the hearing children the teacher wears a microphone so I can hear her. If I don't understand the work I can ask my teacher to explain it in the deaf unit.

Sometimes I like being deaf and sometimes I wish I was hearing. I like being deaf because when I go to bed I take my hearing aid out and I can't hear my mom playing music."

Schools for the Deaf

Special schools for deaf children teach the same subjects as mainstream, public schools but in different ways, using sign language, lip-reading, and technological aids.

Which Language?

At an international conference about educating deaf children in 1880, it was decided not to allow the use of sign language to teach deaf children. Signing was considered an inferior way of communication (only one of the delegates at that conference was deaf). Eventually the ban was lifted in the 1970s, and signing was permitted. The controversy about the best method to teach children who are deaf continues in the 21st century.

There is much debate over the use of language in deaf schools. Some deaf schools only teach using sign language. Others use only oral communication (speech, lip-reading, and aided hearing with hearing aids). Some deaf schools are bilingual, using both methods of communication.

▼ *A teacher and student using sign language to communicate the lesson.*

▲ *Deaf students pause for breath while training. They attend the Alabama Institute for the Deaf and Blind.*

At a deaf school, children do not have to struggle to understand speech. They can mix with other deaf children and share in the richness of the deaf community, culture, and language. However, some people object to special schools. They argue that such schooling does not sufficiently prepare a person for life after school in a hearing world.

Technology in School

Some schools are designed equally for hearing and non-hearing children, taught orally. For instance, the Eduplex Primary School in Pretoria, South Africa, is fitted with devices that pick up speech signals from teachers and transmit them directly to a child's hearing aid. The children hear the teacher's voice, but all of the other noise is not amplified, so the deaf child can concentrate on the teacher and is not distracted by other classroom noises.

CASE NOTES

ANGEL'S STORY

Angel is from Croatia and is now 38. He was born deaf in a hearing family. He attended mainstream schools and is now studying at the University of Zagreb. Angel is also a gym teacher at the School for the Deaf in Zagreb. He plays for the Croatian deaf handball team, which won a gold medal in the Deaflympics in Melbourne in 2005 and in Rome in 2001.

"Many deaf children have to do a lot of homework to catch up on what they didn't understand during the day at school. Deaf children also miss out on a lot of information that seems so normal to other children, they don't understand cartoons, fairy tales... I have often been distressed because I didn't understand what characters on TV were saying.

The main problem for deaf children here in Croatia is accessible education; adjusting methods to their needs and making information accessible. From my perspective, the needs of almost all deaf children are the same: education in their own language—sign language. When I attended regular school, there was no sign language. I didn't understand much. I just sat there, pretending to follow what the teacher and other pupils were saying, and dreaming.

It's not fair that deaf children and their parents have so many worries and obstacles from so early on. This affects the quality of their childhood and their life."

Deafness and Adulthood

Hearing difficulties or deafness should not be a barrier to work, socializing, or participating fully in society.

From actors to politicians, people who are deaf today work successfully in many different fields. For instance, the actress Marlee Matlin, who is almost completely deaf, has starred in many films and popular television series and has won several major awards for her acting skills.

"It is important that deaf people and deaf performers are visible on television and in the media. There's lots of ignorance and misinformation about deaf people, their language and culture— and drama is an effective way of raising issues, of educating and challenging audiences."
David Horbury, television producer

At Work
According to a report published by the Royal National Institute for the Deaf, more than a third of deaf or hard of hearing people are unemployed. However, it is not difficult to make a workplace suitable for someone with no, or limited, hearing. These measures can be taken:

• placing the work station in a central position so the deaf worker can see everyone and feel less isolated

• providing communication support in meetings— perhaps with a loop system for hearing aid users (see page 33)

• having textphones (see page 32) and vibrating pagers

• ensuring the fire alarm system has flashing lights

• providing deaf awareness training for other staff.

". . . relatively small adjustments can make a big difference to integrating deaf and hard of hearing people into the workplace."
Susan Anderson, Royal National Institute for the Deaf

EVELYN'S STORY

Dame Evelyn Glennie is a world famous percussionist. She has composed hundreds of pieces and performed and collaborated with a huge range of other musicians from Bjork to Sting. Evelyn Glennie is also profoundly deaf. Becoming deaf at 12 years of age did not dampen her musical ambitions.

"Deafness does not mean that you can't hear, only that there is something wrong with the ears. Even someone who is totally deaf can still hear/feel sounds…. My hearing is something that bothers other people far more than it bothers me. There are a couple of inconveniences, but in general it doesn't affect my life much. For me, my deafness is no more important than the fact I am female with brown eyes. Sure, I sometimes have to find solutions to problems related to my hearing and music, but so do all musicians. Most of us know very little about hearing, even though we do it all the time. Likewise, I don't know very much about deafness, what's more I'm not particularly interested."

At Play

Most sports activities pose no problem to people with hearing difficulties. Television programs and films are subtitled for the deaf and hard of hearing. Deaf people can also watch and participate in theater and concert performances. Many thousands of deaf people enjoy deaf raves. Deaf raves were started in the UK by a DJ who is totally deaf. Lights change color in time with the music, the bass and beat of which can be felt through the floor. There are often signing performers and stand-up comedians too.

▶ *Percussion soloist Evelyn Glennie rehearses before a performance.*

◀ *Marlee Matlin won an Academy Award for Best Actress in 1987 in the film* Children of a Lesser God.

explaining... DEAFNESS

Technology

Scientists are constantly developing new forms of technology that make it easier for deaf people to communicate with each other and with hearing people. The Internet and other innovations have also increased the opportunities for communication.

Alarms

We live in a world dominated by sound. Spoken words are largely used for communication; sounds such as buzzes, alarm bells, and sirens warn of danger. Many deaf people can legally drive, but in some countries, deaf people are not allowed to drive, because they cannot hear alerts such as an ambulance siren or a horn beeping. However, many cars can be fitted with special devices that light up when a particular sound is heard, alerting the driver to its source and cause.

Noises that alert a person to certain information can often be replaced with flashing lights or movement. For example, a doorbell can flash and an alarm clock can vibrate. One small, portable, vibrating beeper can be set to combine all these alarms.

Moreover, some hearing dogs are trained to alert their owners to particular sounds. If a phone rings or an alarm goes off, the dog nudges his or her owner and leads them to the source of the sound.

On the Phone

Special telephones can convert sounds into a series of beeps which are relayed over the phone line and translated into text on a printer or word processor. A recent invention, called Synface, helps someone who is hard of hearing to use a hearing telephone (with a computer screen attached). The machine transforms the spoken word into corresponding facial and lip movement on a computerized face that appears on screen. This allows the listener who is hard of hearing to use lip-reading skills as well as any limited hearing.

◄ *A hearing dog can be recognized by a specially-colored jacket and lead. Around 70 percent of hearing dogs are rescued from animal shelters.*

▲ *With the Synface system, the face on the computer screen "translates" spoken words into facial movements to help the viewer follow the conversation.*

Instant Communication

TalkbyText and Skype are two systems that allow instant two-way typed conversation between callers in real time. Such systems are used by hearing people to communicate too.

Scientists are developing a program that converts spoken and written English into American Sign Language. A virtual character, or avatar, will show signs on a computer or cell phone screen.

Typetalk

Typetalk is a telephone service for deaf people. A trained operator links a deaf user on a textphone (a specially adapted telephone with a keyboard) and a hearing person on a regular telephone. A person who is deaf types a message, which the operator reads to the hearing person. The operator then types the other caller's reply.

Noise Reduction

Some people with hearing difficulties find it hard to filter out background noises such as coughing, humming fans, or people whispering. To reduce this noise, induction loops provide a direct link between the sound source (for instance a person on stage in a theater) and the hearer (his or her hearing aid or a special receiver).

Invisible infrared light can carry sound to special hearing receivers. Sound (from a person's voice) is processed in a machine and then sent to an infrared radiator which sends the light over the listening area to the receiver.

Deafness and the Family

When a person is diagnosed as deaf or hard of hearing, it can have a huge impact upon a family. If most other members of the family are not deaf, the deafness will create challenges in everyday communication.

A child who is deaf and who is born to deaf parents will be able to follow their chosen method of communication, most likely sign language. However, fewer than 10 percent of deaf children are born to deaf parents.

▼ *The members of this family are all deaf. They communicate using sign language.*

Hearing parents who have a deaf child may worry about how they will communicate with their child as he or she grows older. Many people struggle to learn sign language, just as they may struggle to learn another language. They may feel torn between the pressure to integrate their child into the predominantly hearing world, while acknowledging the support and identity of the deaf community.

CHOOSING A DEAF BABY

In 2002, a deaf couple in Maryland, chose to have a deaf baby. To create a "designer baby," the egg is fertilized outside the woman's body. The embryos are then screened to see if there are genes present which cause deafness (and other conditions). The selected embryos are implanted in the mother's womb where they develop naturally. This procedure has caused a lot of controversy.

Some people believe that deaf parents should be able to select an embryo to ensure they have a deaf child who can be included in the deaf community. In some places, however, this would be against the law.

▲ *A mother and her daughter practice sign language together.*

"My dad never got involved in conversations. He'd wander off saying none of us spoke properly and we all mumbled. Then he'd make some reference to a conversation that happened a while ago. When we called him, he never answered. He really got cross when my mom said he should get a hearing test because he said there was nothing wrong with him and he was still young. Eventually he got his hearing tested and guess what, he did need a hearing aid."
Aiter, age 15

A New Language

Sudden deafness presents many issues. Other family members must suddenly develop new ways to communicate. In a mainly hearing family, a deaf child may literally struggle to be heard. Everyone in the family must work to find ways of communicating that do not exclude anyone. This may involve learning a new language (sign language) and changing many patterns of behavior, such as talking without facing a person or shouting up the stairs to get someone's attention.

Fighting Discrimination

For centuries, deaf people have been persecuted and badly treated. In Europe, until the middle of the eighteenth century, deaf people who could not speak were not recognized by the law as people and were not allowed to marry.

For a long time, a person who was deaf had little status in society. People who could not hear were considered to be less intelligent than others. Often, as there was no recognized way to communicate with a deaf person, he or she was wrongly diagnosed with mental health problems, and sent to institutions, such as mental asylums. Today, however, a person who is deaf has the same rights as a hearing person.

Legal Rights

There are laws in many countries to protect the rights of any person with a disability. A person who is deaf or hard of hearing has a right to be educated, to work and to enjoy a full life in society. These laws are often difficult to enforce, however. It is important that everyone works to make sure that each person, whatever his or her hearing ability, has the opportunity to participate fully in society.

Around the World

How deaf people are treated by laws and society varies drastically from one country to another.

• In developing countries, fewer than 1 in 40 people who would benefit from a hearing aid have one.

• 80 percent of deaf people live in low- and middle-income countries.

• 50 percent of deafness is avoidable through prevention, early diagnosis and management.

Many organizations, including the World Health Organization, are working to help reduce the incidence of deafness. This can be achieved by immunizing (protecting) children against diseases, such as mumps, that can cause deafness, and by making sure that children who have severe ear infections receive medical care before it causes deafness.

Other organizations, such as the charity Hands Around the World, are working to support the deaf in these countries by providing hearing aids to people who need them so they can live and work in society, just like anyone else.

The Deaf Community

The Deaf, written with a capital D, is sometimes used to describe people who are deaf and feel strongly that they are part of the Deaf Community. They do not regard deafness as a disability. In their opinion, it is society that disables Deaf people by

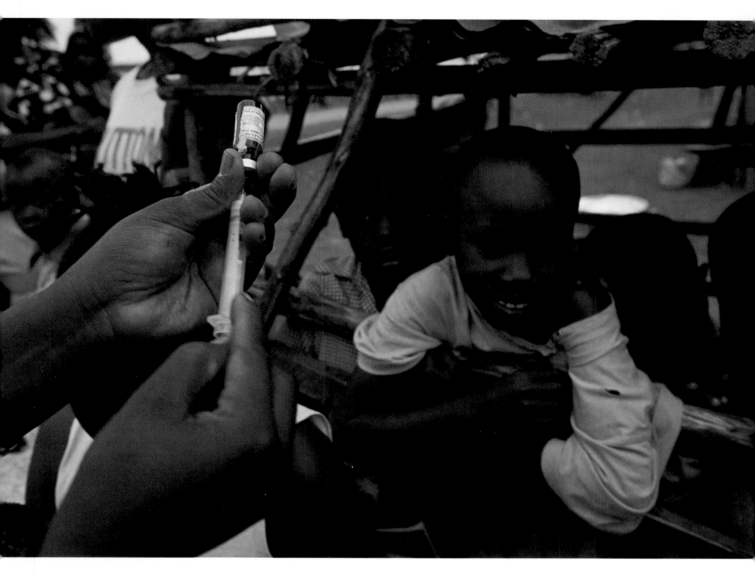

not providing proper access for them. For instance, a Deaf person is disabled because society does not provide a signer or captions in a movie theater.

Does deafness need to be treated or "corrected?" Many Deaf people are very opposed to "treating" deafness with devices such as cochlear implants or hearing aids, especially for children. They believe that being Deaf is about belonging to a cultural and

▲ *Children wait in line to receive measles vaccinations in Kenya. Measles can cause permanent deafness.*

linguistic minority. They believe that Deaf people should not need to become hearing, but that people who hear should learn to communicate clearly with the Deaf, using sign language. They believe that hearing implants or aids threaten and undermine sign language and Deafness.

The Future for Deafness

Scientists and doctors are constantly investigating all aspects of deafness, from understanding the causes to discovering new treatments.

Genetic Research

Genetic research is a key area for scientists to find ways to reverse the effects of deafness, especially when caused by damaged hair cells. Scientists have discovered some of the genes involved in the healthy development of hair cells. They are continuing to identify these genes so that in the future, they can be used to heal damaged cells.

"It is now a question of when—not if— we cure deafness."
Deafness Research UK

Treating Otosclerosis

A common cause of deafness is otosclerosis, which causes abnormal bone growth in the middle ear (see page 15). Until now, this condition has been treated by using surgery to replace the bones. However, researchers have now identified a gene that causes the condition. They have begun to look into ways of controlling the gene to prevent the condition.

Stem Cells

Stem cells are cells which are able to divide and become many different types of cells. Researchers have found some stem cells in the inner ear of mammals. They are looking into ways of making these stem cells into hair cells. So far the research has only been carried out on mice, but if it is successful, stem cells could be transplanted into a human cochlea where they could become healthy hair cells.

Brainstem Implants

Cochlear implants cannot help a person who has a damaged auditory nerve. Recent advances in technology have enabled doctors to carry out

▲ *Auditory brainstem response equipment being operated by an audiologist. This equipment is used to screen for diseases of the acoustic nerve.*

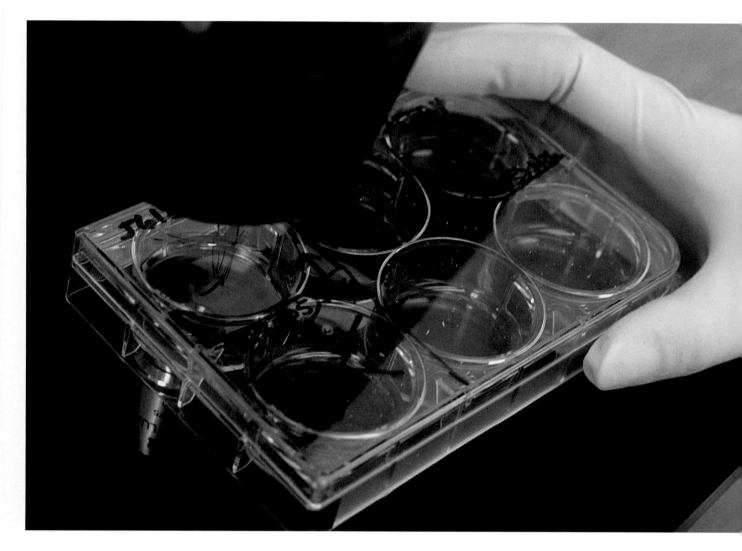

▲ *A scientist examines stem cells under a microscope. Scientists hope that stem cell research may change the future for people whose deafness is caused by damaged hair cells.*

auditory brainstem implants. These inserts are shaped like pencil tips and consist of electrodes that stimulate nerves so that a person can hear certain frequencies. People with auditory brain stem implants wear an external receiver and speech processor. This device converts sounds into electrical signals, which are then sent to the implant.

Tinnitus

Researchers have discovered that overproduction of a protein in the brain, called glutamate, may be responsible for some cases of tinnitus. If so, there could be a new drug to counter this.

New Hearing Aids

As well as medical advances, technological advances have transformed hearing aids. Modern hearing aids can look more like designer accessories than a hearing aid.

Glossary

amplify to make louder

auditory to do with hearing

auditory nerve the nerve that leads from the ear to the part of the brain that processes sounds

audiologist a person who performs and analyzes hearing tests

audiogram a graph showing the measurement of hearing levels

cochlea a snail-shaped organ in the inner ear filled with fluid

conductive hearing loss hearing impairment caused by problems in the path from the outer ear to the inner ear

controversy a subject that causes disagreement

Deaflympics an international sports competition organized especially for deaf athletes since 1924

decibel the measurement of how loud a sound is

delegate a person who represents an organization at a meeting

developing countries countries where many people are poor and do not have easy access to health care

diagnosis identification of a particular condition, such as deafness

discrimination treating someone differently or allowing them fewer opportunities and fewer rights than other people

electrodes electrical conductors through which an electric current can pass

embryo an unborn fetus that is still developing

energy the capacity for something to do work or move

finger spelling a system which uses hand shapes to spell separate letters of the alphabet

fetus a baby before it is born

frequency the pitch of a sound. It can be high or low

Gaelic the language of the Celts who lived in Scotland

gene the basic unit of heredity by which characteristics are passed from one generation to the next

genetic research investigating how an understanding of genes provides ways of preventing or curing illnesses

glue ear condition in which fluid builds up in the middle ear, causing hearing loss

hearing dogs specially trained dogs that alert their deaf owners to sounds such as doorbells, babies crying, or alarms

implant an object which is inserted permanently inside something

induction loop a magnetic loop that transmits sounds to hearing aids within a certain distance

integrate to mix in, to become a part of a group

language acquisition process of learning and using a language

linguistic to do with language

membrane a thin layer of material or tissue

meningitis swelling in a part of the brain caused by an infection that can cause headaches, fever, sensitivity to light, stiff muscles and, in severe cases, death

ossicles the three tiny bones in the middle ear, known as the hammer, anvil, and stirrup, which amplify sound

otosclerosis a condition that causes the bones in the middle ear to harden or grow abnormally

pager a one-way electronic device that beeps to warn a person when someone is trying to contact them

partially deaf a person with some hearing

perforated pierced with a hole

phonetically teaching children the letters of the alphabet not by their names, but by how they sound

profoundly deaf a person who can only hear sounds above 95 decibels

real time when things happen at the same time as they are done, without a delay

rubella a disease that is a mild form of measles, and is also known as German measles

sensorineural hearing loss hearing impairment caused by damage between the inner ear and brain

sign language a language which uses hands, facial expressions, and movements instead of sounds

textphone machine that allows you to type a conversation down a telephone line

tinnitus ringing or buzzing noise in the ears, caused by loud noise, ear infections, objects, or growths in the ear, or by ear wax. Tinnitus can be a permanent condition

womb an organ in the lower body of a woman where babies grow and develop

Further Information

Books

Deaf People Around the World : Educational Perspectives, Donald F. Moores and Margery S. Miller, *Gallaudet University Press*, 2009

Hands of My Father : a Hearing Boy, his Deaf Parents, and the Language of Love, Myron Uhlberg, *Bantam Dell*, 2009

Language and Deafness, Peter V. Paul, *Jones and Bartlett*, 2009

Signs and Voices : Deaf Culture, Identity, Language, and Arts, Kristin A. Lindgren, Doreen DeLuca, and Donna Jo Napoli, editors.
Gallaudet University Press, 2008

Films

The Miracle Worker
Playfilm Productions, 1962
The story of Helen Keller.

Organizations

Alexander Graham Bell Association for the Deaf
www.agbell.org
(202) 337-5220 Voice
(202) 337-5221 TTY

American Sign Language Teachers Association
http://www.aslta.org

American Society for Deaf Children
http://deafchildren.org
1-866-895-4206 Voice

Canadian Cultural Society of the Deaf
www.ccsdeaf.com

Council on Education of the Deaf
www.deafed.net

International Center on Deafness and the Arts
www.icodaarts.org
(847) 509-8260 Voice
(847) 509-8257 TTY

Laurent Clerc National Deaf Education Center
http://clerccenter.gallaudet.edu
(202) 651-5031 Voice
(202) 651-5636 TTY/Video Phone

National Association of the Deaf
www.nad.org
(301) 587-1788 Voice
(301) 587-1789 TTY

National Theatre of the Deaf
www.ntd.org
(860) 236-4193 Voice
1-800-NTD-1967   Video Phone

Registry of Interpreters for the Deaf
www.rid.org
(703) 838-0030 Voice
(703) 838-0459 TTY

Web Sites

American Sign Language Demonstrations
www.lifeprint.com

Hearing Aids Guide
www.healthyhearing.com

Note to Parents and Teachers: Every effort has been made by the publishers to ensure that these web sites are suitable for children, that they are of the highest educational value, and that they contain no inappropriate or offensive material. However, because of the nature of the Internet, it is impossible to guarantee that the contents of these sites will not be altered. We strongly advise that Internet access is supervised by a responsible adult.

Index

Titles and Contents in Explaining . . .

Explaining Asthma

What is Asthma? • History of Asthma • Increase in Asthma • Who has Asthma? • Healthy Lungs • How Asthma Affects the Lungs • What Triggers Asthma? • Asthma and Allergies • Diagnosing Asthma • Preventing an Attack • Relieving an Attack • What to Do During an Attack • Growing Up with Asthma • Living with Asthma • Asthma and Exercise • Asthma Treatments

Explaining Autism

What is Autism? • Autism: A Brief History • The Rise of Autism • The Autistic Spectrum • The Signs of Autism • Autism and Inheritance • The Triggers of Autism • Autism and the Body • Autism and Mental Health • Can Autism Be Treated? • Living with Autism • Autism and Families • Autism and School • Asperger Syndrome • Autism and Adulthood • The Future for Autism

Explaining Blindness

What is Blindness? • Causes and Effects • Visual Impairment • Color Blindness and Night Blindness • Eye Tests • Treatments and Cures • Coping with Blindness • Optical Aids • On the Move • Guide Dogs and Canes • Home Life • Blindness and Families • Blindness at School • Blindness as an Adult • Blindness, Sports, and Leisure • The Future for Blindness

Explaining Cerebral Palsy

What is Cerebral Palsy? • The Causes of Cerebral Palsy • Diagnosis • Types of Cerebral Palsy • Other Effects of Cerebral Palsy • Managing Cerebral Palsy • Other Support • Technological Support • Communication • How It Feels • Everyday Life • Being at School • Cerebral Palsy and the Family • Into Adulthood • Raising Awareness • The Future

Explaining Cystic Fibrosis

What is Cystic Fibrosis? • Cystic Fibrosis: A Brief History • What Causes Cystic Fibrosis? • Screening and Diagnosis • The Effects of Cystic Fibrosis • How is Cystic Fibrosis Managed? • Infections and Illness • A Special Diet • Clearing the Airways • Physical Exercise • Cystic Fibrosis and Families • Cystic Fibrosis at School • Growing Up with Cystic Fibrosis • New Treatments • The Future

Explaining Deafness

What is Deafness? • Ears and Sounds • Types of Deafness • Causes of Deafness • Signs of Deafness • Diagnosis • Treating Deafness • Lip Reading • Sign Language • Deafness and Education • Schools for the Deaf • Deafness and Adulthood • Technology • Deafness and the Family • Fighting Discrimination • The Future for Deafness

Explaining Diabetes

What is Diabetes? • Diabetes: A Brief History • Type 1 Diabetes • Type 2 Diabetes • Symptoms and Diagnosis • Medication • Hypoglycemia • Eyes, Skin, and Feet • Other Health Issues • Healthy Eating and Drinking • Physical Activity • Living with Diabetes • Diabetes and Families • Diabetes at School • Growing Up with Diabetes • Diabetes Treatment

Explaining Down Syndrome

What is Down Syndrome? • Changing Attitudes • Who has Down Syndrome? • What are Chromosomes? • The Extra Chromosome • Individual Differences • Health Problems • Testing for Down Syndrome • Diagnosing at Birth • Babies with Down Syndrome • Toddlers with Down Syndrome • At School • Friendships and Fun • Effects on the Family • Living Independently • The Future

Explaining Epilepsy

What is Epilepsy? • Causes and Effects • Who has Epilepsy? • Partial Seizures • Generalized Seizures • Triggers • Diagnosis • How You Can Help • Controlling Epilepsy • Taking Medicines • Living with Epilepsy • Epilepsy and Families • Epilepsy at School • Sports and Leisure • Growing Up with Epilepsy • Epilepsy Treatments

Explaining Food Allergies

What are Food Allergies? • Food Allergies: A Brief History • Food Aversion, Intolerance, or Allergy? • What Is an Allergic Reaction? • Food Allergies: Common Culprits • Anaphylaxis • Testing for Food Allergies • Avoiding Allergic Reactions • Treating Allergic Reactions • Food Allergies on the Rise • Food Allergies and Families • Food Allergies and Age • Living with Food Allergies • 21st Century Problems • Treatment for Food Allergies